STEM

The Remarkable RINGED PLANETS

Problem Solving with Variables

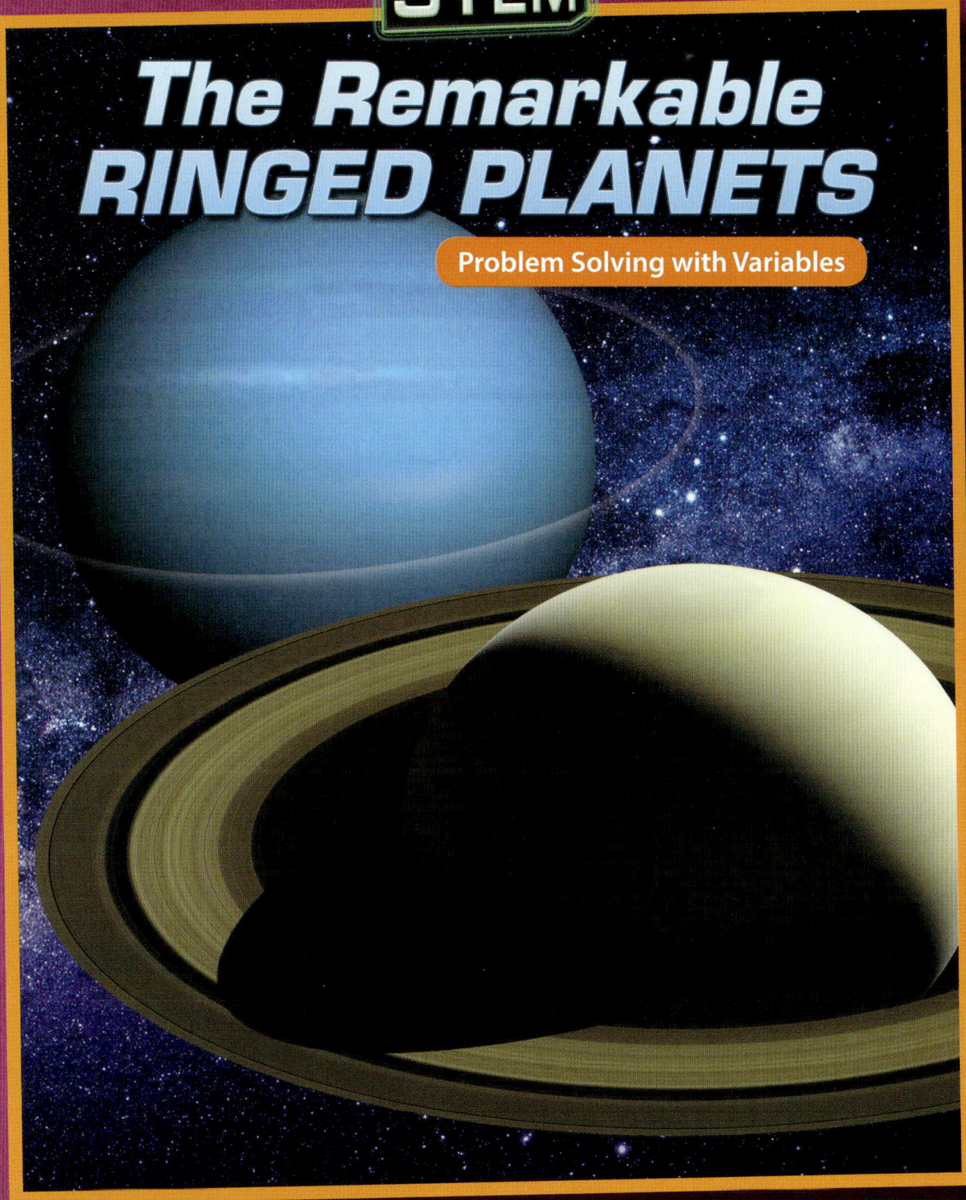

Angela Davids

Contributing Author

Alison S. Marzocchi, Ph.D.

Consultant

Colleen Pollitt, M.A.Ed.
Math Support Teacher
Howard County Public Schools

Publishing Credits

Rachelle Cracchiolo, M.S.Ed., *Publisher*
Conni Medina, M.A.Ed., *Editor in Chief*
Dona Herweck Rice, *Series Developer*
Emily R. Smith, M.A.Ed., *Series Developer*
Diana Kenney, M.A.Ed., NBCT, *Content Director*
Stacy Monsman, M.A., *Editor*
Michelle Jovin, M.A., *Associate Editor*
Fabiola Sepulveda, *Graphic Designer*
Lee Aucoin, *Sr. Graphic Designer*

Image Credits: front cover (bottom), back cover, p.9 (all), p.12 NASA; p.5 Larry Landolfi/ Science Source; pp.6–7 David Hardy/Science Source; p.8 Lynette Cook/Science Source; p.10 (left), p.18 National Maritime Museum; p.10 (right) Haags Historisch Museum; p.11 (bottom left) Prisma Archivo /Alamy; p.11 (bottom center and right) National Academy of Sciences; p.13 (insert) NASA/JPL/Space Science Institute; p.13 NASA/ JPL-Caltech; p.14 Mark Garlick/Science Photo Library/Newscom; p.16 National Air and Space Museum/Smithsonian; p.17 (top left and right, middle, and bottom), p.21 (both), p.24 (left) NASA/JPL; p.19 (bottom left) Wellcome Library, London; p.19 (bottom center) Dibner Library of the History of Science and Technology; p.19 (bottom right) Public Domain/Wikimedia; p.20 NASA/JPL/USGS; p.22 NASA/Jet Propulsion Laboratory/Caltech; pp.22–23 NASA, ESA, and D. Calzetti (University of Massachusetts); p.23 NASA/MIT/TESS; p.24 (right) NASA/Joel Kowsky; p.25 (top) NASA/MSFC/David Higginbotham; p.25 (bottom) Maggie Masetti/Flickr; p.26 Gianni Tortoli/Science Source; p.27 Meinzahn/iStock; p.31 Science Source; all other images from iStock and/or Shutterstock.

Library of Congress Cataloging-in-Publication Data

Names: Davids, Angela, 1973- author.
Title: The remarkable ringed planets : problem solving with variables / Angela Davids.
Other titles: At head of title: STEM
Description: Huntington Beach, CA : Teacher Created Materials, [2019] | Audience: Grades 4 to 6. | Includes bibliographical references and index. | Identifiers: LCCN 2018051876 (print) | LCCN 2018054808 (ebook) | ISBN 9781425855314 (eBook) | ISBN 9781425858872 (pbk. : alk. paper)
Subjects: LCSH: Planetary rings--Juvenile literature. | Outer planets--Juvenile literature. | Variables (Mathematics)--Juvenile literature.
Classification: LCC QB603.R55 (ebook) | LCC QB603.R55 D38 2019 (print) | DDC 523.9/8--dc23
LC record available at https://lccn.loc.gov/2018051876

Teacher Created Materials
5301 Oceanus Drive
Huntington Beach, CA 92649-1030
www.tcmpub.com

ISBN 978-1-4258-5887-2

Printed in Malaysia
Thumbprints.21254

Table of Contents

A Universe to Discover

This ancient stone inscription shows the sun, the moon, and Venus.

Since prehistoric times, people have looked up and wondered what is beyond Earth. What is in the night sky? How does it affect people on Earth? The fascination began early. **Archaeologists** have found carvings in stones and bones that date as far back as 32,000 BC. These carvings show that ancient people tracked changes in the moon. Throughout history, people have studied the stars and the planets to know when to plant crops or when to travel to seek food. They used stars to navigate over land and across seas. Scientists still look beyond Earth to learn more about the universe. They have learned that while Earth has only one moon, some planets have none and some have over 50. One area some scientists are now studying is the rings of the planets.

When most people think of a planet with rings, they get a clear image of Saturn in their heads. Those rings were discovered by **astronomer** Galileo Galilei in 1610. Hans Lippershey of the Netherlands is credited with the invention of the telescope in 1608; however it was Galileo who made the invention—and Saturn—famous. But there are three other planets in our solar system with rings. Imagine the amazement of astronomers and **physicists** when they saw spacecraft photos that proved there were rings around other planets. The scientists were brimming with questions. How many rings do each of these planets have? What are the rings made of? How old are the rings? Scientists got to work to find out.

LET'S EXPLORE MATH

Imagine that a scientist observes three planets through a telescope. She estimates the number of moons each planet has and records her findings on number lines.

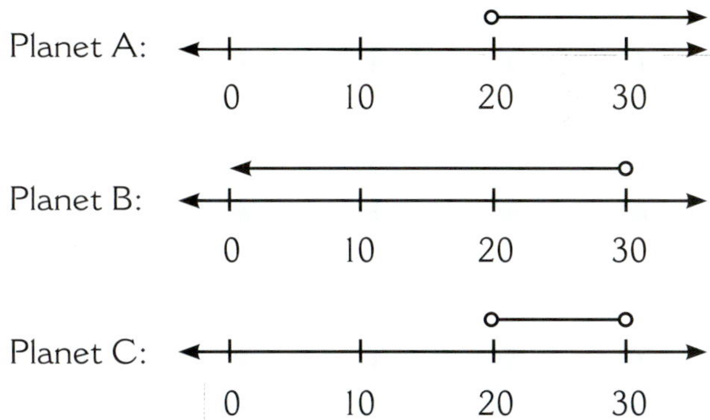

1. Write two inequalities to represent the number of moons Planets A and B have. Use *m* to stand for the number of moons.
2. What do you know about the number of moons Planet C has?

Jupiter: Planet King

Jupiter is the largest planet in our solar system. Its name comes from the highest god in Roman mythology. It is easily recognized by its giant red spot. The spot is a windstorm of gases that swirl at 400 miles (644 kilometers) per hour. Astronomers first saw that famous spot by telescope in the 1600s. It took almost four hundred more years for scientists to discover Jupiter's rings. Finally, in 1979, the *Voyager 1* spacecraft was sent into space by the National Aeronautics and Space Administration (NASA). Photos from that trip showed scientists Jupiter's rings for the first time.

How Big Is Big?

Jupiter is massive! All the planets in our solar system can fit inside of it at one time. Jupiter is like a huge gumball machine that can hold more than 1,300 Earths. It measures almost 273,000 mi. (440,000 km) around at its **equator**. In comparison, Earth is 24,900 mi. (40,073 km) around. That means someone would have to travel around Earth more than 10 times to equal the distance of traveling around Jupiter once.

Jupiter is the fifth farthest planet from the sun. It is about five times farther from the sun than Earth is. As Jupiter and Earth travel around the sun, they move closer and farther away from one another. Earth and Jupiter are almost 400 million mi. (644 million km) apart when they are at their closest point during **orbit**.

LET'S EXPLORE MATH

Jupiter has the shortest day in the solar system. One day, defined as the time it takes for Jupiter to **rotate** once, is only about 10 hours. Choose all the expressions that represent the number of hours that pass on Jupiter when *d* days have passed.

A. $10d$

B. $24d$

C. $\frac{d}{10}$

D. $d \times 10$

E. $5d + 5d$

Jupiter can be called a cousin of the sun. About 4.5 billion years ago, gas and dust created a cloud that would form the sun and the rest of the solar system. The sun was made from much of this cloud, and the planets came from the leftovers. Jupiter's **atmosphere** makes up most of the planet, since Jupiter does not have a firm "ground" like Earth does. Like the sun, Jupiter is mostly made up of hydrogen, followed by helium and other gases. However, the sun is a star, not a planet. Though Jupiter is made up of the same gases as stars, it never grew large enough or hot enough to create the energy of a star.

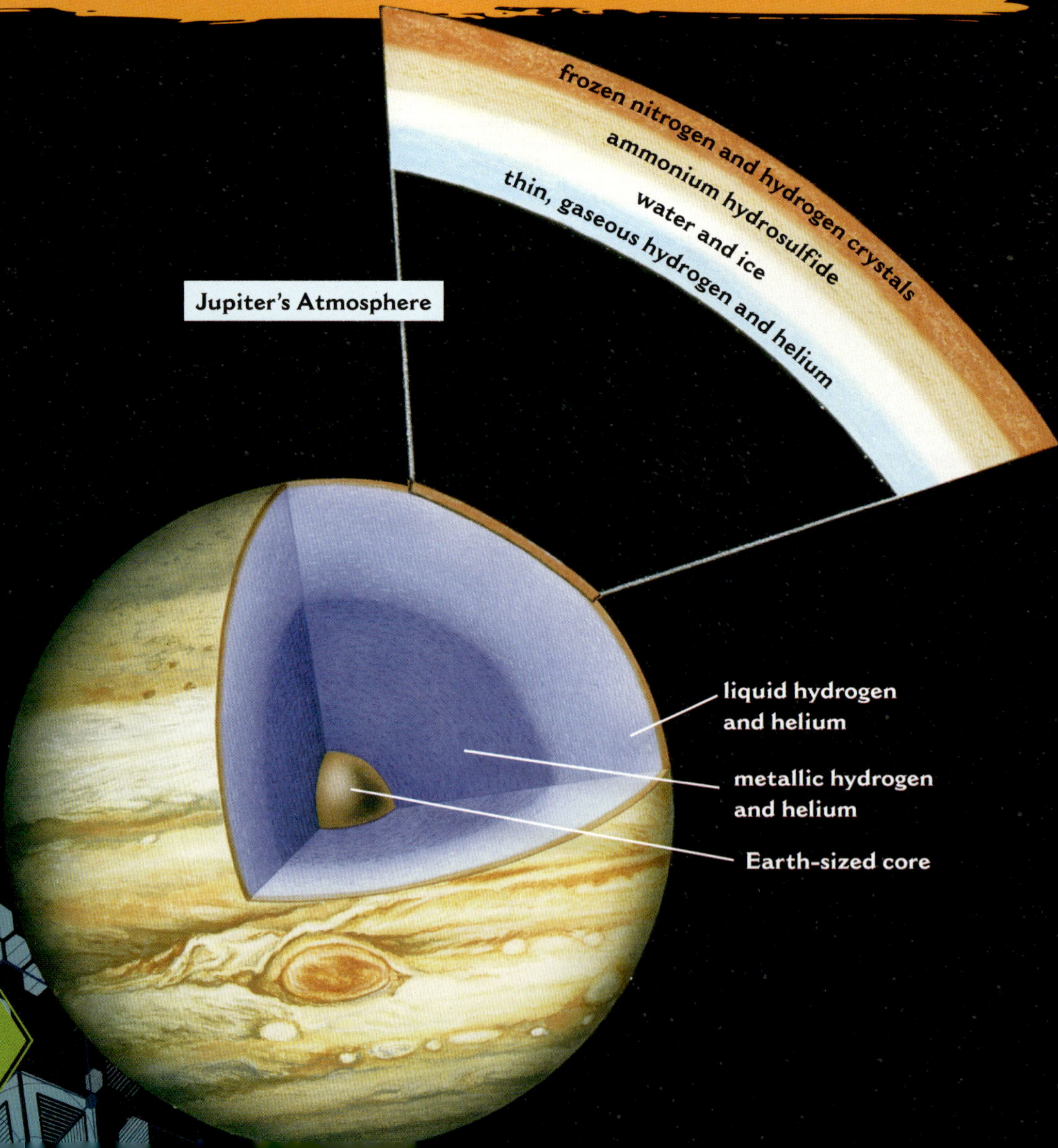

Surprise! It Has Rings!

NASA first launched a spacecraft to Jupiter in 1972. But, it was a 1979 photo from the *Voyager 1* spacecraft that captured Jupiter's thin rings. Everyone was shocked. The dust **particles** that form the rings appeared only when they were backlit by the sun. The *Galileo* spacecraft that orbited Jupiter from 1995 to 2003 gathered new data. It showed that **meteoroids** were colliding into Amalthea, Thebe, Adrastea, and Metis—the closest of Jupiter's 79 moons. Dust from these collisions is what created Jupiter's four rings. Scientists call the two outer rings *gossamer rings* and the thick inner ring the *halo*. The ring in between those is called the *main ring*.

Jupiter's Rings and Moons

This photo of Jupiter's rings was taken by the *Galileo* spacecraft.

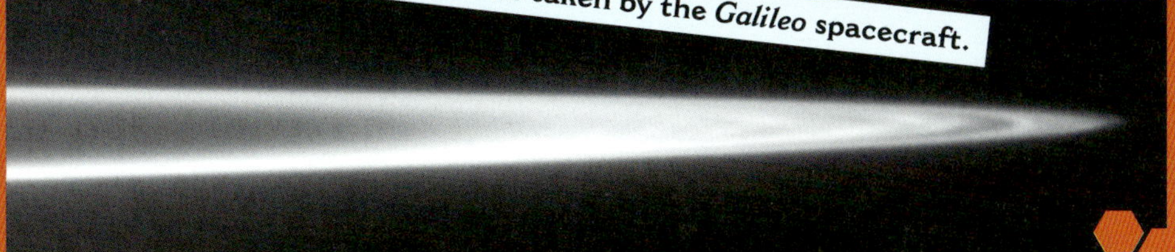

Saturn: The Most Famous Rings of All

Galileo's drawing

Saturn's rings have been a mystery for more than four hundred years. It began in 1610, when the most famous astronomer in history spotted them. Through his telescope, Galileo saw a large circle with two smaller circles on each side. His best guess was that Saturn had a moon to the left and a moon to the right. He made his next discovery in 1612, when these "moons" seemed to disappear. Two years after that, Galileo discovered that the objects had returned. This time, he described them as handles or arms. In 1616, Galileo drew Saturn with a thick ring around it.

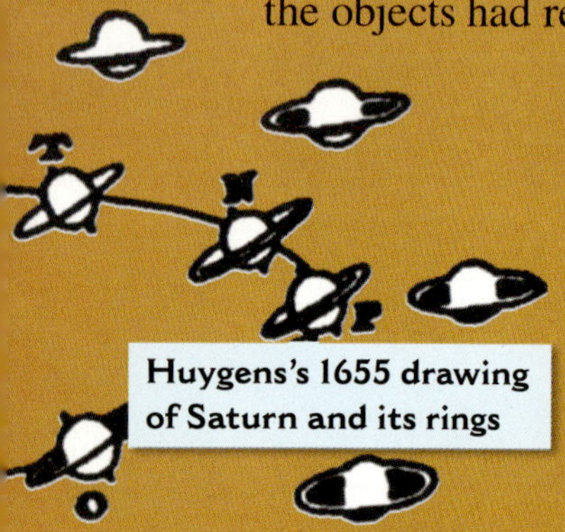

Huygens's 1655 drawing of Saturn and its rings

The next detective in the great mystery of Saturn's rings is Christiaan Huygens (HOY-gunz). By 1655, telescopes could help people see much farther. With a telescope he designed, Huygens saw Saturn's rings clearly. They were not attached to Saturn as some believed. When Huygens saw the rings, he thought they were solid. For about two hundred years, most scientists agreed.

In the mid-1800s, a few astronomers questioned Huygens's theory. They noted that they could see through Saturn's rings, so the rings could not be solid. Next, physicist James Clerk Maxwell wrote an essay about his opinion. He said two centuries of observations showed that the rings had changed in size. Therefore, they could not be solid. In 1895, astronomers William Campbell and James Keeler confirmed that the rings are actually made up of many small particles.

Galileo Galilei 1610

Christiaan Huygens 1655

LET'S EXPLORE MATH

Saturn's distance from the sun is farther than Earth's. To determine Saturn's distance from the sun, a scientist writes the equation $s = 9.5e$.

1. What do the variables s and e mean?
2. What does 9.5 mean?
3. What operation does the scientist indicate?

James Clerk Maxwell

William Campbell

James Keeler

1859

1895

Four spacecraft have orbited Saturn. The *Cassini-Huygens* is the most recent, which launched in 1997 to study the planet, its moons, and its rings. It made it to Saturn in 2004. Photographs revealed a sea of **methane** gas on Titan, one of Saturn's moons. Scientists also learned there are water vapor **geysers** on another of Saturn's moons, Enceladus.

Before *Cassini-Huygens*, scientists already knew that Saturn's rings were made mostly of particles of ice, plus some rock and dust. They had observed that pieces of the rings could be small like grains of salt or as large as buildings. But *Cassini-Huygens* showed scientists that the rings are constantly moving. Gravity pulls the particles into seven distinct rings, so from Earth they appear stationary. *Cassini-Huygens* showed that the rings can ripple like waves and the edges can twist up or down.

Scientists still disagree on how the rings formed. Some say that any of Saturn's moons could have collided with each other or that **asteroids** and meteoroids crashed into the moons. Then, the **debris** from these collisions formed the rings. Other scientists believe that those pieces of debris might rejoin to form new moons, so the particles wouldn't spread far enough to enter the rings. Scientists cannot be sure how the rings were made. Did they form with our solar system 4.5 billion years ago? Probably not. Data from the *Cassini-Huygens* mission say that Saturn's rings may be as young as 100 million years old. Saturn never stops surprising everyone!

This colorized photo of Saturn's C-ring (blue) and B-ring (yellow) was taken by the *Voyager 2* spacecraft.

This photo taken by *Cassini-Huygens* shows Enceladus' water vapor geysers.

This illustration shows the *Cassini-Huygens* passing by Saturn.

Uranus: The Tilted Planet

In 1781, William Herschel became the first person to determine that Uranus (YUR-uh-nuhs) was a planet. At first, he thought it was either a comet or a star, like many other people did. By making more detailed observations of its orbit through a telescope, he concluded that it was a planet. Since the planet was nearly invisible to the bare eye, it was the first one to be discovered since ancient times. Herschel quickly became famous for his discovery. Johann Elert Bode confirmed it was a planet in 1783. Uranus was almost named after King George III. It would have been called Georgium Sidus. Instead, the planet was named after the Greek sky god.

Uranus is 4.5 billion years old. It is easy to identify in photos because of its bluish-green color and pale rings. The planet's 13 rings are made mostly of dust. It takes 84 Earth years for Uranus to orbit around the sun. Winter at its north pole is 21 years of darkness, and summer is 21 years of light. Like Earth, the spring and fall have both daytime and nighttime in a single day. Each day (one rotation) lasts 17 hours and 14 minutes.

This illustration shows how the particles that make up Uranus' rings would look up close.

LET'S EXPLORE MATH

Uranus' **radius** is about 4 times wider than Earth's. Use the bar model to answer the questions.

u			
e	e	e	e

1. Write an equation relating Uranus' radius (u) to Earth's radius (e).
2. Earth's radius is about 6,371 kilometers. How wide is Uranus' radius? Find your solution using the equation and the bar model.

Uranus has 5 major moons, 22 lesser moons, and 13 rings.

Uranus' 13 rings are tilted at about a 90-degree angle, just like the planet is. People may imagine Earth's equator looking like a belt around a pair of pants. Uranus' equator looks more like a Ferris wheel. Scientists have long wondered why Uranus is tilted. Some believe that two or more objects crashed into Uranus and pushed it on its side. An older theory is that an Earth-sized object (or maybe even larger) collided with Uranus. A collision may also be why this planet rotates from east to west instead of west to east like all other planets (except for Venus). No one is sure what really happened.

A team of scientists in Australia first discovered several rings around Uranus in 1977. However, most of what is known about the planet comes from *Voyager 2*—the only spacecraft to fly near there. It took *Voyager 2* nine years to pass Uranus. It took about 5.5 hours to fly by Uranus and the spacecraft provided information about its weather, the surfaces of its moons, and its rings. *Voyager 2* also took thousands of photos that continue to amaze scientists.

Recently, NASA proposed a new flight to Uranus and Neptune, the two planets farthest from the sun. Scientists believe that these two planets may have been closer to the sun once. But something happened and they moved away about four billion years ago. NASA thinks a new flight could help scientists learn more about how the solar system formed and changed.

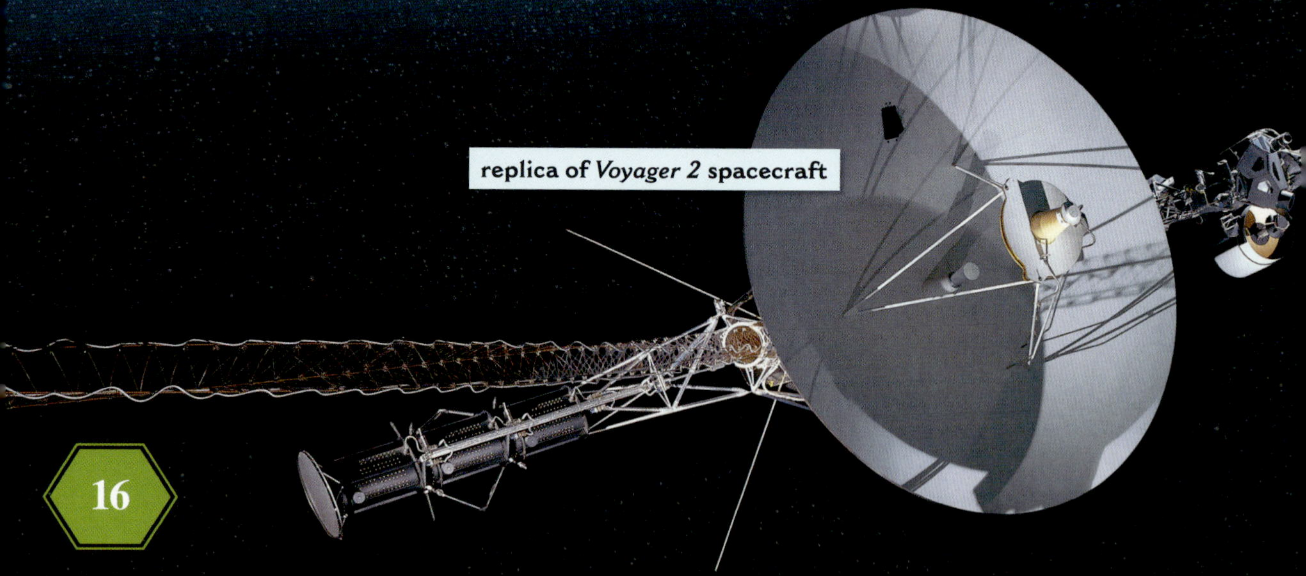

replica of *Voyager 2* spacecraft

Voyager 2 took these photos of three of Uranus' major moons—Oberon (top), Miranda (left), and Titania (bottom)—in 1986.

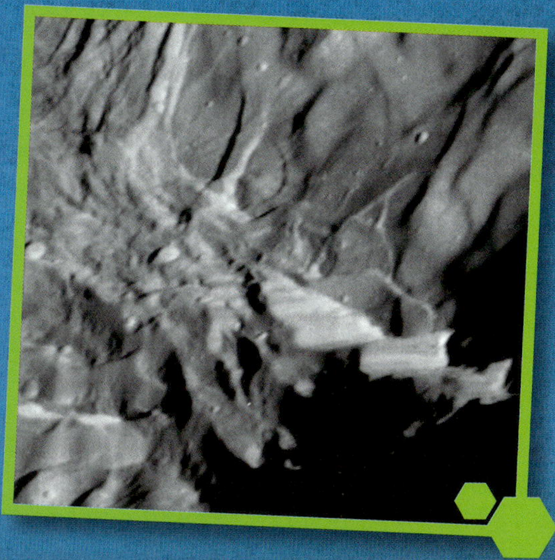

NASA scientists assigned different colors to this photo to represent different parts of Uranus' atmosphere.

Neptune: The Ice Planet

Four astronomers helped discover Neptune. First, Italian astronomer Galileo sketched Neptune's position in the sky. Looking into his small telescope, he guessed it was a star. Scientists didn't learn anything new about Neptune for more than two hundred years.

In the United Kingdom, astronomer John Couch Adams worked on a complex math problem about the path Uranus takes around the sun. In France, Urbain-Jean-Joseph Le Verrier was doing the same thing. The two men did not know they were working on the same problem. They both came up with the same answer. Both thought there could be a large, unknown planet pulling on Uranus. That planet's **gravitational force** could cause Uranus to go off track. Adams and Le Verrier took their theory and used it to make new predictions. Each thought he knew where to find the mystery planet.

The Moment of Discovery

Adams shared his findings but did not publish them because his colleagues didn't think they were important. Meanwhile, Le Verrier sent his calculations to German astronomer Johann Gottfried Galle. Based on Le Verrier's calculations, Galle easily found Neptune in one day. He is the person given credit for its discovery. The date was September 23, 1846.

Galileo Galilei

1610

John Couch Adams — Urbain-Jean-Joseph Le Verrier — Johann Gottfried Galle

1845

1846

This computer-generated montage shows how Neptune would appear as a spacecraft approaches Triton.

An Unusual Moon

Neptune's discovery quickly led to another. William Lassell was an amateur astronomer. He found the moon Triton just over two weeks after Galle discovered Neptune. Triton is the largest of Neptune's 13 confirmed moons. Triton is similar in size to the dwarf planet Pluto. There is evidence that this moon may actually have been a large mass that Neptune pulled in with its gravity. Now, it circles Neptune in the opposite direction that Neptune rotates. It is the only large moon in our solar system that does that. Astronomers didn't find another one of Neptune's moons for 103 years.

NASA's *Voyager 2* made the next big discovery in 1989 when, after 12 years in space, it became the only spacecraft to fly by Neptune. The 2.9 billion mi. (4.7 billion km) trip was worth it! Thanks to *Voyager 2*, scientists discovered five new moons and four rings. They also found that Triton is the coldest known planetary body in the solar system. It is so cold that Triton has volcanoes that spew out chunks of ice instead of molten lava!

This *Voyager 2* image shows Neptune's outermost ring clumping into three arcs.

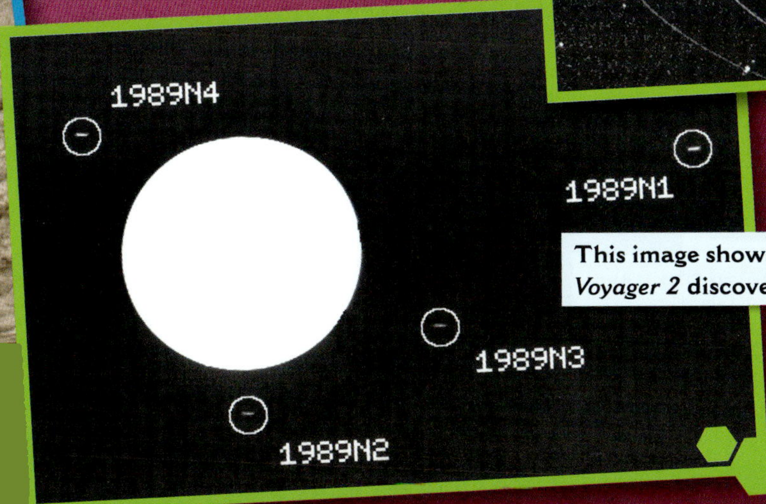

This image shows four of the five moons *Voyager 2* discovered around Neptune.

The Future of Exploration

Imagine the thrill for the thousands of space scientists who continue to seek and discover. They are busy preparing for missions that are planned. They are also researching ideas for missions they want to do.

In April 2018, NASA sent a **satellite** (called TESS) into space to capture when stars dim. When stars temporarily seem to lose some brightness, the cause can be a planet orbiting that star. The TESS satellite can capture photos of over 200,000 stars at a time! Scientists expect to locate more than 1,500 new planets from this satellite's two-year mission.

Missions to Jupiter and Saturn

The *Europa Clipper* is a proposed mission to search for proof of living things on one of Jupiter's moons, Europa. **Microscopic** organisms might be living in Europa's icy ocean. If living things can survive there, there could be life on other moons and planets. Scientists say this could be the closest we will come to finding the answer.

Artists at NASA created this travel poster imagining life on Europa.

Researchers have also proposed five trips to Saturn. One of those, called SPRITE, would dive into Saturn's atmosphere. The mission would last just 90 minutes. Scientists hope to learn about what gases are in Saturn's atmosphere. This and other data could help in understanding how the solar system formed.

The TESS satellite took this image of more than 200,000 stars.

LET'S EXPLORE MATH

Scientists expect to locate more than 1,500 new planets using the TESS satellite.

1. Write an inequality to represent the situation. Use p to stand for the number of new planets.
2. Graph the inequality on a number line like this one.

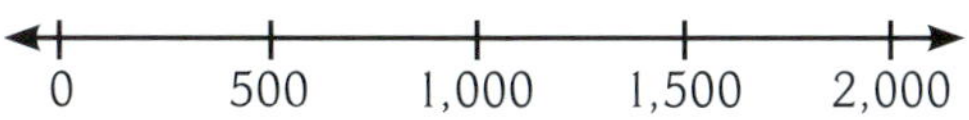

3. **a.** What are three values that make the inequality true?

   b. What are three values that make the inequality untrue?

Missions to Neptune and Uranus

Since Neptune and Uranus are so far away, scientists don't know as much about these planets as they do about others. Just one mission, *Voyager 2*, has flown by these planets. Scientists want to know how these icy planets formed. They want to learn more about their rings. By studying one or both of these planets, more can be learned about how and why our solar system exists. One idea is to have a spacecraft fly by the planets closely and quickly. Another proposal is to have a ship dive directly into Uranus' atmosphere to gather information. The atmosphere would destroy the ship, but the data captured would give scientists information they can use for decades.

Voyager 2 image of clouds in Neptune's atmosphere

Dr. Bonnie Buratti and Dr. Fran Bagenal speak about *Voyager 2*'s Neptune mission and the future of space travel.

The James Webb Space Telescope

Some of the most detailed space exploration will be with the world's largest space telescope. Scheduled to be launched in spring 2021, the James Webb Space Telescope can monitor more than one hundred objects at once. For up to a decade, it will search for the first **galaxies** created after the **big bang**. Scientists hope to learn how galaxies were created. Also, the telescope will search through dust clouds to find stars and planets that are just starting to form.

Engineer Dave Chaney inspects the six primary mirrors on the James Webb Space Telescope.

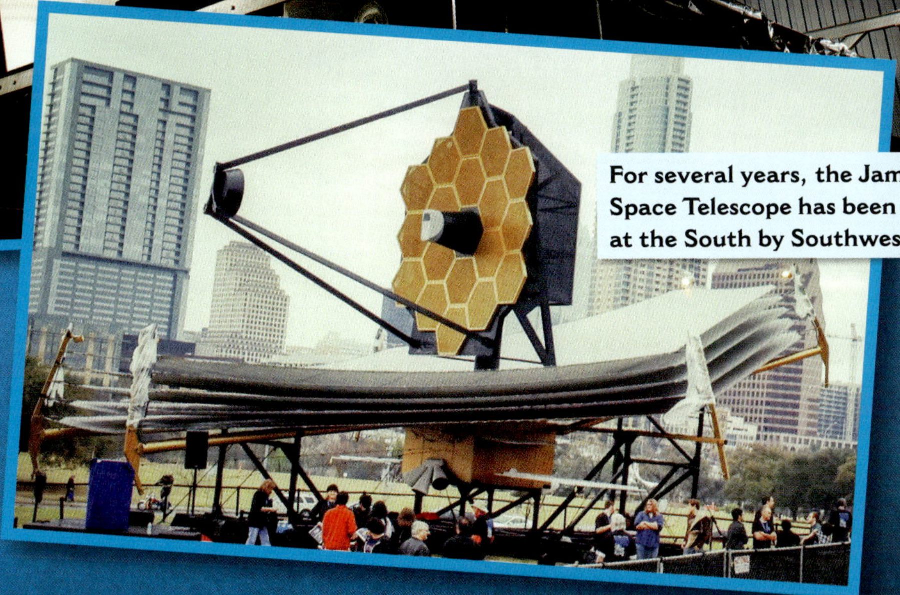

For several years, the James Webb Space Telescope has been on display at the South by Southwest Festival.

The Search Never Ends

People have always looked to the skies. And they have been fascinated by what they could see and what they couldn't see. Many discoveries were made hundreds of years ago using basic telescopes. Think of all the possibilities scientists can discover today using new technology. Scientists work hard to make telescopes that can see deeper into space. They design spacecraft that can travel farther. Satellites and the internet let scientists share pictures and videos instantly. Then they work together.

Looking beyond Earth is thrilling! You can learn more about the solar system right now. Visit an **observatory**. Use the telescopes there to see stars, planets, and even the rings around the planets. Ask lots of questions—the people who work at observatories want to share their passion for space with everyone.

If there isn't an observatory near you, join an astronomy club or become an amateur astronomer. Some amateur astronomers and clubs even make their own telescopes to monitor the skies!

There's always more to learn about our solar system and galaxy. The universe is always expanding. Keep learning to expand your "space sense" and never stop exploring!

Galileo's telescope

A man looks at the Zeiss Telescope at the Griffith Observatory.

LET'S EXPLORE MATH

Imagine that students in a school's astronomy club spotted 120 different stars last semester. This semester, they spot 20 additional stars at each meeting.

1. Write an equation to represent the total number of stars spotted. Use s to stand for the total number of stars and m to stand for the number of meetings.
2. How many total stars have been spotted after the sixth meeting?

Problem Solving

The sun is actually a giant star. Scientists are studying whether there might be more giant stars in the universe that are similar to our sun. Imagine that Dee, Frank, and Giovanna are scientists who discover a new giant star. Each scientist spots a new planet orbiting this star. They give their research notes to their assistants, using g to stand for Giovanna's planet, f to stand for Frank's planet, and d to stand for Dee's planet.

The scientists request that the assistants draw a map showing their discoveries. Use the research notes to draw a possible map on graph paper, with circles representing the giant star and planets and points representing moons. Let 1 unit on the graph paper stand for 10,000 kilometers. Then, use the equations, inequalities, and numbers of kilometers to write a summary for the scientists, proving that your map is a reasonable possibility.

Giant Star

- There is a giant star in the middle of the new system.

Distances

- Frank's planet is twice as far from the giant star as Dee's planet.
- The distance of Giovanna's planet from the giant star is represented by $g > f + d$.

Sizes

- The radius of Dee's planet is represented by $d = \frac{1}{3}f$.
- Giovanna's planet's radius is two times the radius of Dee's planet.

Moons

- The number of moons that Dee and Giovanna's planets have are related by $d > g$.
- The number of moons that Frank's planet has is represented by $f = d + 2$.

Glossary

archaeologists—people who study materials that cultures leave behind

asteroids—thousands of small, rocky bodies that circle around the sun

astronomer—a person who studies stars, planets, and other objects in outer space

atmosphere—the whole mass of gases that surround a planet or star

big bang—a huge expansion that might have happened when the universe began

debris—the pieces left behind after something has been destroyed

equator—an imaginary circle around the middle of a planet that is equidistant from the north and south poles

galaxies—large groups of stars that make up the universe

geysers—springs that shoot out hot water and steam

gravitational force—a force that pulls two objects toward each other

meteoroids—small chunks of rock or iron that travel through space

methane—an odorless, colorless gas

microscopic—something so small that it can only be seen with a microscope

observatory—a special building for studying stars, planets, weather, and more

orbit—the curved path that something (such as a planet) follows around something else (such as the sun)

particles—very small pieces of something

physicists—people who study matter and energy and how they interact

radius—the distance from the center of a circle to any point on the circle

rotate—move in a circular motion around a point

satellite—an object in space that orbits another object

Index

Answer Key

Let's Explore Math

page 5

1. **Planet A:** $m > 20$;
   Planet B: $m < 30$
2. Planet C has between 20 and 30 moons.

page 7

A, D, E

page 11

1. Saturn's distance from the sun is s; Earth's distance from the sun is e.
2. Saturn's distance from the sun is 9.5 times farther than Earth's.
3. multiplication

page 15

1. $u = 4e$
2. 25,484 km

page 23

1. $p > 1500$
2. 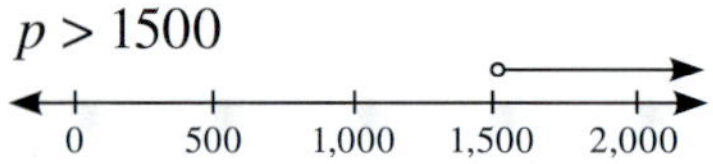

3. **a.** Examples: *1,501*; *1,600*; *2,000*

   b. Examples: *0*; *5*; *1,250*. Values less than 0 are not realistic for the situation.

page 27

1. $s = 120 + 20m$
2. 240 stars

Problem Solving

Answers should include a map and justification of the map's accuracy. Example: *The giant star is in the middle of the system. Frank's planet is 40,000 km away from the giant star (20,000 × 2 = 40,000) and Giovanna's planet is 70,000 km away from the giant star (70,000 > 40,000 + 20,000). Dee's planet's radius is 10,000* $\frac{1}{3}$ × *30,000 = 10,000). Giovanna's planet's radius is 20,000 km (2 × 10,000 = 20,000). Dee's planet has 2 moons (2 > 1). Frank's planet has 4 moons (2 + 2 = 4).*

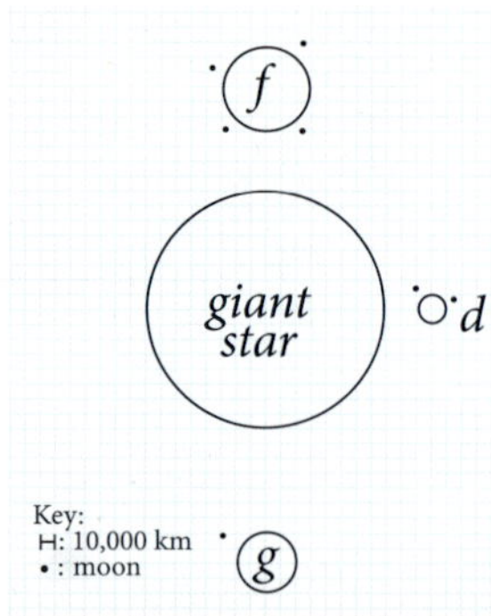